The Essential
ROASTING TIN
COOKBOOK

A Quick Start Guide
To
Roasting Tin
Cooking

Over 80 Easy And Delicious
One Dish, No-Fuss Oven Recipes

First published in 2018 by Erin Rose Publishing

Text and illustration copyright © 2018 Erin Rose Publishing

Design: Julie Anson

ISBN: 978-1-911492-28-3

A CIP record for this book is available from the British Library.

DISCLAIMER: This book is for informational purposes only and not intended as a substitute for the medical advice, diagnosis or treatment of a physician or qualified healthcare provider. The reader should consult a physician before undertaking a new health care regime and in all matters relating to his/her health, and particularly with respect to any symptoms that may require diagnosis or medical attention.

While every care has been taken in compiling the recipes for this book we cannot accept responsibility for any problems which arise as a result of preparing one of the recipes. The author and publisher disclaim responsibility for any adverse effects that may arise from the use or application of the recipes in this book. Some of the recipes in this book include nuts and eggs. If you have an egg or nut allergy it's important to avoid these.

CONTENTS

The Essential Roasting Tin Cookbook

INTRODUCTION

Healthy and delicious tray baked meals are winners! Not only are they super-simple to make but they take little preparation and cut down on the washing up too!

We don't always have time to plan meals or spend ages cooking but still want wholesome, nutritious, meals so roasting tin recipes are ideal.

Anyone who is a fan of one-pot recipes will enjoy tossing a few ingredients into a roasting tin or oven-proof dish, popping it in the oven and enjoying a great tasting, no-fuss dinner.

There is something for everyone and the recipes are laid out in sections for breakfast, main meals and sweet treats. You can choose from simple recipes like, sausage & apple bake, lemon chilli chicken, halloumi & sweet potato bake or various roast vegetable, fish dishes and low carb lasagne which make lovely mid-week family meals. There are delicious recipes for lazy Sunday breakfasts using traditional store-cupboard ingredients and nutritious grains and fruit.

Using a roasting tin, baking tray or oven-proof dish and some basic ingredients you'll have a wide range of recipes at your fingertips. Have a store of dried herbs and spices in the cupboard and a few windowsill herbs which will liven up any roasting tin meal, so feel free to make substitutions and come up with your own recipes.

Enjoy finding your favourites!

Breakfast

Raspberry & Quinoa Breakfast Bake

Ingredients

200g (7oz) raspberries
100g (3½ oz) blueberries
50g (2oz) coconut flakes
50g (2oz) quinoa
50g (2oz) oats
3 bananas, sliced

2 eggs
1 tablespoon honey
1 teaspoon vanilla extract
½ teaspoon cinnamon
400mls (14fl oz) milk

SERVES 2

Method

Preheat the oven to 180C/360F. Grease a small rectangular ovenproof dish with butter. In a bowl, whisk together the eggs, milk, honey, cinnamon and vanilla extract. Scatter half of the fruit into the dish then sprinkle the quinoa and oats on top. Make another layer of fruit on top. Pour the egg mixture slowly into the dish. Sprinkle the coconut on top. Transfer it to the oven and bake for around 50 minutes. Serve either hot or cold, with a dollop of yogurt.

Baked Apple & Blackberry Oats

SERVES 2

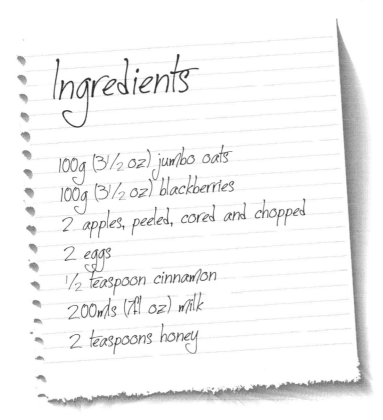

Ingredients

100g (3½ oz) jumbo oats

100g (3½ oz) blackberries

2 apples, peeled, cored and chopped

2 eggs

½ teaspoon cinnamon

200mls (7fl oz) milk

2 teaspoons honey

Method

Preheat the oven to 180C/360F. Scatter the blackberries and apples into a small ovenproof dish. In a bowl, whisk together the milk and eggs and add in the cinnamon, honey and oats and mix well. Pour the milky mixture into the dish and stir well. Transfer it to the oven and bake for around 30 minutes, or until golden. Serve on its own or with a dollop of yogurt. Can be eaten hot or cold..

Apple & Coconut Granola

Ingredients

125g (4oz) almonds, chopped
125g (4oz) chopped walnuts
125g (4oz) chopped pecans
50g (2oz) unsweetened coconut flakes
50g (2oz) pumpkin seeds
50g (2oz) sesame seeds
50g (2oz) ground flaxseeds (linseeds)
1 apple, peeled, cored and finely diced
1 teaspoon cinnamon
120mls (4fl oz) coconut oil, melted
2 tablespoons honey
1/2 teaspoon sea salt

SERVES 4

Method

Line a baking tray with parchment paper. In a bowl, mix together the honey, coconut oil, cinnamon and salt. Place the nuts, seeds, apple and coconut flakes into a large bowl and coat them in the oil mixture. Scatter the ingredients evenly onto the baking tray. Transfer it to the oven, preheated to 150C/300F and cook for 15 minutes then stir the granola. Cook for another 15 minutes or until golden. Allow it to cool then store it in an airtight container. You can eat it on its own as a snack or with nut milk or live yogurt.

Baked Scrambled Eggs

Ingredients

50g (2oz) butter, melted

12 eggs

1/2 teaspoon sea salt

300mls (1/2 pint) milk

**SERVES
6**

Method

Preheat the oven to 180C/360F. Pour melted butter into an ovenproof dish. In a bowl, whisk the eggs and salt. Pour in the milk and whisk some more. Pour the egg mixture into the dish. Transfer it to the oven and bake for 10 minutes. Remove it from the oven and give it a stir with a fork. Return it to the oven and bake for another 10 minutes or until the eggs have set.

Meaty Breakfast Casserole

SERVES
6

Ingredients

275g (10oz) cheese, grated (shredded)

8 sausages, casing removed and crumbled

6 slices of bread, diced

6 large eggs, beaten

400mls (14fl oz) milk

Butter for greasing

Method

Preheat the oven to 180C/360F. Grease an ovenproof dish or small roasting tin with some butter. Toss the sausage meat into a hot frying pan and brown it for a few minutes then add it to the dish. Add in the bread cubes. In a bowl, whisk together the eggs and milk then pour it into the dish, covering the other ingredients. Sprinkle the cheese on top. Cover it with foil. Transfer it to the oven and cook for around 50 minutes or until the eggs have set. This can be prepared the night before, ready to pop in the oven for a hearty breakfast.

Vegetarian Breakfast Casserole

SERVES 8

Ingredients

200g (7oz) button mushrooms

200g (7oz) Cheddar cheese, grated (shredded)

12 eggs

3 carrots, peeled and grated (shredded)

2 handfuls of fresh spinach

2 potatoes, peeled and diced (you could use leftovers too)

1 red pepper (bell pepper), deseeded and chopped

1 teaspoon sea salt

1/4 teaspoon freshly ground black pepper

400mls (14fl oz) milk

1 tablespoon olive oil

Method

Preheat the oven to 190C/380F. Heat the oil in a frying pan. Add the carrots, potatoes, red pepper (bell pepper) and mushrooms and cook for around 7 minutes, until they have softened. Add in the spinach and cook for 2 more minutes. Transfer the ingredients to an ovenproof dish. In a bowl, whisk together the milk and eggs. Season with salt and pepper. Pour the egg into the vegetables. Sprinkle the cheese over the top. Transfer it to the oven and cook for 40-45 minutes, or until golden.

Bacon & Egg Tray Bake

Ingredients

100g (3½ oz) button mushrooms

100g (3½ oz) cherry tomatoes

4 rashers of bacon

2 large handfuls of baby spinach

2 eggs

1 tablespoon olive oil

Sea salt

Freshly ground black pepper

SERVES 2

Method

Preheat the oven to 200C/400F. Pour the oil into a roasting tin or baking tray. Lay out the bacon and add the tomatoes and mushrooms. Transfer it to the oven and cook for 10 minutes. Remove it and turn over the bacon. Make some room at one side of the tin and add in the spinach. Flatten the spinach and make 2 hollows which will hold the eggs. Crack the eggs into the hollows. Season with salt and pepper. Return the tray to the oven and cook for around 5 minutes or until the eggs are set and done to your liking. Serve and eat straight away.

Cheese & Ham Oven Omelette

SERVES
6

Ingredients

100g (3½ oz) cheese, grated (shredded)

75g (3oz) cooked ham, chopped

10 large eggs

1 handful of fresh parsley, chopped

400mls (14fl oz) milk

Butter for greasing

Method

Preheat the oven to 190C/380F. Grease an ovenproof dish with butter. In a bowl, whisk the eggs and then add in the milk. Stir in the ham, cheese and parsley. Pour the egg mixture into the prepared dish. Transfer it to the oven and bake for 40 minutes, or until the eggs are set. Serve and eat straight away.

Chorizo & Tomato Baked Eggs

SERVES
4

Ingredients

400g (14oz) passata or tomato pasta sauce

300g (11oz) cooked potatoes, diced (leftovers are perfect!)

100g (3½ oz) chorizo sausage, sliced

4 eggs

1 tablespoon olive oil

Method

Preheat the oven to 180C/360F. Heat the oil in a frying pan, add the chorizo and cook for 2 minutes. Add in the potatoes and passata/pasta sauce and warm them through. Spoon it into an ovenproof dish. Gently crack each egg on top of the tomato base. Transfer it to the oven and cook for 5 minutes or until the eggs are set and done to your liking. Serve on its own or with fresh crusty bread. Enjoy.

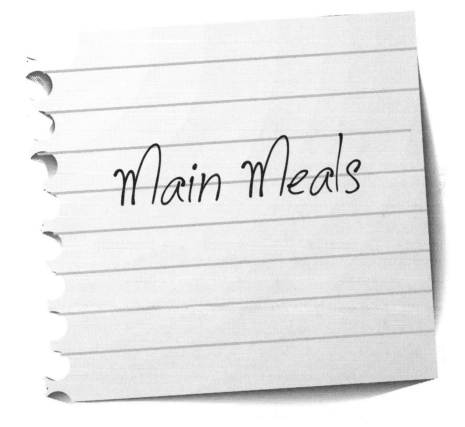

Main Meals

Greek Meatball & Feta Bake

SERVES 4

Ingredients

- 400g (14oz) tin of chopped tomatoes
- 500g (1lb 2oz) passata
- 200g (7oz) feta cheese, crumbled
- 25g (1oz) toasted pine nuts
- 1½ teaspoons ground cinnamon
- 1 teaspoon chilli powder
- 1 small handful of fresh oregano or 1 teaspoon dried oregano
- 4 tablespoons olive oil
- 1 teaspoon honey
- 200mls (7fl oz) red wine

FOR THE MEATBALLS:

- 600g (1lb 5oz) minced lamb
- 75g (3oz) Greek yogurt
- 3 cloves of garlic, chopped
- 2 slices of brown bread, crumbed
- 1 onion, peeled and finely chopped
- 1 teaspoon mixed herbs

Method

Preheat the oven to 170C/340F. Place all the ingredients for the meat balls into a large bowl and mix well. Shape the mixture into individual meatballs. Add the chopped tomatoes, passata, honey, oregano, wine, cinnamon, chilli and olive oil into a roasting tin and mix well.

Place the meatballs into the mixture. Cover the roasting tin with foil. Transfer it to the oven and cook for 90 minutes. Remove the foil and add the feta cheese. Return it to the oven and cook for around 10 minutes. Sprinkle on the pine nuts just before serving. Can be served with pasta, crusty bread, new potatoes or salad.

Sausage Ragu & Spaghetti

Ingredients

- 400g (14oz) spaghetti
- 400g (14oz) tinned chopped tomatoes
- 250g (9oz) cherry tomatoes
- 8 pork sausages, casing removed and crumbled
- 4 garlic cloves, roughly chopped
- 2 tablespoons tomato paste
- 1 small bunch of fresh thyme
- 1 teaspoon chilli flakes
- 250mls (9 fl oz) chicken stock (broth)
- 1 tablespoon olive oil

SERVES 4

Method

Preheat the oven to 220C/440F. Scatter the tinned tomatoes, thyme, chilli, garlic and sausages into an ovenproof dish and drizzle them with olive oil. Transfer them to the oven and cook for 20 minutes. Pour in the stock (broth) and add the cherry tomatoes and tomato paste and stir. Return it to the oven and cook for a further 10-15 minutes or until the tomatoes are soft. In the meantime, cook the spaghetti according to the instructions then drain it. Toss the spaghetti into the ragu and serve.

Chinese Cod Bake

Ingredients

450g (1lb) pak choi, quartered lengthways

8 spring onions (scallions), chopped

4 cod fillets

4cm (2 inch) chunk of ginger, finely chopped

3 garlic cloves, finely sliced

1 red chilli, deseeded and chopped

1 teaspoon sesame seeds, toasted

1/2 a head of cabbage, grated (shredded)

2 tablespoon soy sauce

3 tablespoons sesame oil

1 teaspoon olive oil

Juice of 1/2 a lemon

SERVES 4

Method

Preheat the oven to 220C /440F. Bring a saucepan of water to the boil, lower the pak choi (bok choy) and cabbage into the water and remove it after a minute. Allow it to drain. Pour the sesame oil into a roasting tin, add the pak choi, cabbage, spring onions (scallions), chilli, garlic and soy sauce and mix well. Pour the olive oil into a bowl and add the lemon juice and ginger then coat the cod in the mixture. Place the fish on top of vegetables. Loosely cover the roasting tin with foil. Transfer it to the oven and bake for around 20 minutes or until completely cooked. Sprinkle with sesame seeds before serving.

Cheese, Tomato & Fennel Gratin

SERVES 4

Ingredients

175g (6oz) Cheddar cheese, grated (shredded)

2 x 400g (2 x 14oz) tinned chopped tomatoes

3 fennel bulbs, thinly sliced

2 cloves of garlic, chopped

1 onion, peeled and chopped

1 teaspoon dried mixed herbs

4 tablespoons olive oil

1 teaspoon honey

Method

Preheat the oven to 180C/360F. Scatter the fennel, garlic and onion into a roasting tin and drizzle in the oil. Toss the ingredients well. Transfer it to the oven and cook for 20 minutes. In a bowl, mix together the tomatoes with a teaspoon of honey and the dried mixed herbs. Pour the tomatoes into the roasting tin and return it to the oven for 40 minutes. Scatter the cheese over the bake and cook it in the oven for around 5 minutes or until the cheese begins to bubble. Serve with crusty bread or alongside meat dishes.

Paprika Chicken & Butternut Squash

SERVES 4

Ingredients

125g (4oz) olives, stones removed and halved

8 chicken drumsticks

8 cherry tomatoes

2 large courgettes (zucchinis), cut into chunks

1 teaspoon dried oregano

1 butternut squash, peeled and cut into chunks

1 large handful of fresh spinach leaves

1 teaspoon paprika

1/2 teaspoon cumin

2 tablespoons olive oil

Method

Preheat the oven to 200C/400F. Pour the oil into a roasting tin with the paprika, oregano and cumin and stir. Add in the squash and chicken drumsticks and coat them in the mixture. Transfer the roasting tin to the oven and cook for 40 minutes. Add in the tomatoes, olives, courgettes (zucchini) and spinach leaves and coat them in the oil. Return it to the oven and cook for 10 minutes.

Sausage & Apple Bake

Ingredients

8 large, good-quality sausages

4 large potatoes, peeled and diced

3 apples, peeled, cored and cut into wedges

2 carrots, peeled and cut into chunks

25g (1oz) butter, melted

Several sprigs of thyme

A handful of fresh sage leaves

SERVES 4

Method

Heat the oven to 190C/380F. Place the sausages, potatoes, carrot and apple into a roasting tin and add the butter. Season with salt and pepper. Add the thyme and sage leaves and stir the ingredients well. Transfer the roasting tin to the oven and cook for 30-35 minutes or until the sausages and potatoes are completely cooked.

Sea Bass & Ratatouille

Ingredients

4 sea bass fillets

4 cloves of garlic, chopped

1 yellow pepper (bell pepper), chopped

1 red pepper (bell pepper), chopped

1 large courgette (zucchini), chopped

1 aubergine (eggplant), chopped

1 teaspoon dried mixed herbs

1 tablespoon olive oil

1 large handful of fresh basil leaves, chopped

Sea salt

Freshly ground black pepper

SERVES 4

Method

Place the courgette (zucchini) aubergine (eggplant), peppers, garlic, mixed herbs and oil, into an ovenproof roasting dish and toss them well. Season with salt and pepper. Transfer it to the oven and cook at 200C/400F for 25 minutes. Add in half of the fresh basil and stir the vegetables. Place the fish on top of the vegetables. Return it to the oven and cook for 10-12 minutes or until the fish is completely cooked and flakes off.

Baked Figs, Prosciutto & Blue Cheese

SERVES
4

Ingredients

100g (3½ oz) prosciutto, roughly chopped

100g (3½ oz) blue cheese, crumbled

8 fresh figs, quartered

2 tablespoons honey

Method

Preheat the oven to 180C/360F. Scatter the figs and prosciutto into an ovenproof dish. Sprinkle on the cheese and drizzle the honey over the top. Transfer it to the oven and bake for around 15 minutes or until slightly browned. Serve and enjoy.

Hake & Fennel Bake

Ingredients

450g (1lb) new potatoes, halved

25g (1oz) butter, flaked

4 hake fillets

1 fennel bulb, cut into wedges

1 bunch of fresh parsley, finely chopped

2 teaspoons paprika

1 lemon, quartered

150mls (5fl oz) hot vegetable stock (broth)

1 tablespoon olive oil

SERVES
4

Method

Preheat the oven to 200C/400F. Scatter the potatoes and fennel into a roasting tin. Pour the stock (broth) into the tin and add the butter, paprika and parsley. Mix well. Transfer it to the oven and cook for 30 minutes or until the potatoes have softened. Coat the fish in a tablespoon of olive oil then lay it in the roasting tin and return it to the oven. Cook for around 15 minutes, or until the fish is completely cooked. Serve with a wedge of lemon.

Mozzarella & Pesto Flatbread Pizza

SERVES
2

Ingredients

6 sundried tomatoes, drained

2 slices mozzarella cheese, torn

2 flatbread

4 teaspoons pesto

1 tablespoon pine nuts

Pinch of cayenne pepper

Method

Preheat the oven to 200C/400F. Spread some pesto onto each flatbread. Sprinkle the pine nuts on top and add the tomatoes. Top if off with the mozzarella pieces. Season with cayenne pepper. Lay the flatbread in a large roasting tin or baking sheet if you need more space. Transfer it to the oven and cook for 7-8 minutes. Or until the cheese is bubbling. Serve and eat straight away.

Chicken Tikka & Roast Vegetables

Ingredients

FOR THE CHICKEN:

- 4 chicken breasts
- 2.5cm (1 inch) chunk of fresh ginger root, finely chopped
- 1 clove of garlic, crushed
- 1 teaspoon chilli powder
- 1 teaspoon curry powder
- ½ teaspoon sea salt
- ½ teaspoon turmeric
- 125g (4oz) plain (unflavoured) Greek yogurt
- 1 tablespoon olive oil
- Juice of 1 lemon

FOR THE VEGETABLES:

- 1 large aubergine (eggplant) cut into thick chunks
- 4 large tomatoes, de-seeded and cut into chunks
- 1 red pepper (bell pepper), chopped
- 1 yellow pepper (bell pepper) chopped
- 1 tablespoon olive oil
- 1 handful fresh coriander (cilantro), chopped

SERVES 4

Method

For the chicken; place the chilli, salt, curry powder, turmeric, ginger, garlic, yogurt, olive oil and lemon juice into a bowl and stir it well. Coat the chicken in the mixture. Place the vegetables in a large ovenproof dish and coat them in a tablespoon of olive oil. Make a space in the centre of the dish for the chicken breasts or place them on top. Transfer the dish to the oven and cook at 180C/360F for around 35 to 40 minutes or until the chicken is cooked through. Scatter the chopped coriander (cilantro) over the top and serve.

Salsa Verde Chicken

Ingredients

450g (1lb) small new potatoes
350g (12oz) asparagus spears, trimmed
25g (1oz) Parmesan cheese, grated
4 chicken breasts
4 cloves of garlic, chopped
2 slices white bread
2 tablespoons basil, chopped
2 tablespoons fresh parsley, chopped
2 tablespoons fresh tarragon, chopped
1 tablespoon capers, drained
Zest of 1 lemon
3 tablespoons olive oil

SERVES 4

Method

Preheat the oven to 200C/400F. Scatter the potatoes and 3 cloves of garlic into a large roasting tin and coat it in 2 tablespoons of olive oil. Transfer it to the oven and cook for 20 minutes. In the meantime, place the bread, herbs, a clove of garlic, capers and a tablespoon of olive oil into a food processor and blitz to combine them. Combine the breadcrumb mixture with the lemon zest and parmesan. Spread the mixture onto the chicken breasts. Add the chicken to the roasting tin. Return it to the oven and cook for 10 minutes. Add the asparagus and continue cooking for around 10 minutes or until the chicken is cooked through. Season and serve.

Salmon & Olive Bake

Ingredients

- 900g (2lb) baby potatoes, quartered
- 450g (1lb) courgettes (zucchinis), roughly chopped
- 2 x 400g (2x14oz) tins chopped tomatoes
- 100g (3½ oz) black olives
- 4 salmon fillets
- 1 onion, roughly chopped
- 2 tablespoons fresh basil
- 2 tablespoons fresh parsley
- 1 tablespoon olive oil

SERVES 4

Method

Preheat the oven to 200C/400F. Put the potatoes into a roasting tin and coat them in olive oil. Transfer them to the oven and cook for 15 minutes. Add the onion and courgette (zucchini) to the roasting tin and return it to the oven. Cook for a further 15 minutes. Add the tinned tomatoes, olives, basil and parsley to the roasting tin. Lay the salmon fillets on top. Return the roasting tin to the oven and cook for 12-15 minutes or when the salmon is completely cooked. Serve and enjoy!

Low Carb Courgette Lasagne

Ingredients

- 450g (1lb) turkey mince (ground turkey)
- 450g (1lb) cottage cheese
- 2 x 400g (2 x 14 oz) tinned chopped tomatoes
- 250g (9oz) mozzarella cheese, grated (shredded)
- 25g (1oz) Parmesan cheese, grated (shredded)
- 5 courgettes (zucchinis) cut into thin strips
- 1 egg
- 2 handfuls of fresh spinach
- 1 teaspoon dried oregano
- 1 teaspoon dried basil
- 1 teaspoon garlic powder
- 1 tablespoon honey
- 1 tablespoon olive oil
- Sea salt
- Freshly ground black pepper

SERVES 8

Method

Lay the courgette (zucchini) slices onto kitchen roll and sprinkle with salt. Set aside for 15 minutes then squeeze it between the sheets of kitchen roll to remove any excess moisture. Heat the oil in a large pan, add the turkey, herbs and garlic. Cook for 5 minutes, then add the tomatoes, honey and spinach. Bring it to the boil then remove it from the heat. Season with salt and pepper. In a bowl, combine the cottage cheese and egg. Preheat the oven to 180C/360F. Spoon some of the tomato mixture into the bottom of an ovenproof dish. Place a layer of courgette strips on top. Spoon a layer of the tomato mixture on top followed by a layer of cottage cheese. Repeat for the remaining mixture. Finish with a layer of courgette on top, then sprinkle the mozzarella and Parmesan cheese over it. Cover it with foil. Transfer it to the oven and cook for 40 minutes. Remove the foil, return to the oven and cook it for another 15 minutes. Serve with heaps of fresh green salad.

Spiced Chicken & Couscous

Ingredients

12 skinless chicken thighs

2 tablespoons medium curry powder

2 tablespoons paprika

5 cloves of garlic, finely chopped

4 tablespoons olive oil

450g (1lb) couscous

600mls (1 pint) hot chicken stock (broth)

50g (2oz) sultanas

50g (2oz) butter, diced

1 large handful of fresh coriander (cilantro), roughly chopped

SERVES 4

Method

Preheat the oven to 200C/400F. Pour the oil into an ovenproof dish. Add the curry powder, paprika and garlic. Add the chicken and coat it in the spices. Transfer it to the oven and cook it for 30 minutes or until the chicken has completely cooked. In the meantime, put the couscous into a separate ovenproof dish and add the stock (broth). Let it stand for 5 minutes until the stock (broth) has been absorbed. Add the butter and sultanas to the couscous. Cover the couscous with foil and place it in the oven to keep warm until the chicken is done. Sprinkle the coriander (cilantro), over the couscous. Serve the couscous onto plates and add the chicken on top. Eat straight away.

Baked Pesto Chicken

Ingredients

600g (1lb 5oz) new potatoes, quartered
250g (9oz) cherry tomatoes
100g (3½ oz) pesto
4 chicken breasts
4 garlic cloves, chopped
2 courgettes (zucchinis), roughly chopped
2 tablespoons olive oil
A small handful of fresh basil leaves, chopped.

SERVES 4

Method

Preheat the oven to 200C/440F. Scatter the potatoes and garlic into a roasting tin and drizzle with olive oil. Spread some pesto onto each of the chicken breasts and lay them in the roasting tin. Season with salt and pepper. Transfer it to the oven and cook for around 20 minutes. Add the courgettes (zucchinis) and tomatoes to the roasting tin and continue cooking for around 25 minutes or until the chicken is completely cooked. Serve with a sprinkling of chopped basil.

Lemon Chicken & Orzo Pasta

SERVES 4

Ingredients

- 250g (9oz) orzo pasta
- 20 pitted olives, roughly chopped
- 12 chicken thighs
- 2 onions, peeled and roughly chopped
- 2 cloves of garlic, chopped
- 1 lemon, quartered
- 1 handful fresh parsley, chopped
- 200mls (7fl oz) chicken stock (broth)
- 1 tablespoon olive oil
- Sea salt
- Freshly ground black pepper

Method

Preheat the oven to 190C/380F. Place the chicken thighs, garlic and olive oil into an ovenproof dish. Squeeze the lemon over the chicken and place the lemon quarters around it. Add the onion and pour in the stock (broth). Season with salt and pepper. Transfer it to the oven and cook for 45-50 minutes or until the chicken has cooked through and browned. While the chicken is cooking, cook the orzo according to the instructions and drain it. When the chicken is done, add in the olives, parsley and orzo and stir well Serve and eat straight away.

Mexican Quinoa Casserole

Ingredients

- 2 x 400g (2 x 14oz) tins of chopped tomatoes
- 400g (14oz) tin of black beans, drained and rinsed
- 175g (6oz) cheese, grated (shredded)
- 175g (6oz) quinoa
- 125g (4oz) sweetcorn
- 2 cloves of garlic, finely chopped
- 1 tablespoon olive oil
- 1 onion, finely chopped
- 1 green pepper (bell pepper), deseeded and finely chopped
- 1 courgette (zucchini), diced
- ½ teaspoon ground cumin
- 1 teaspoon oregano
- 1 teaspoon paprika
- 1 teaspoon chilli powder
- Juice of ½ lime
- 400mls (14fl oz) vegetable stock (broth)

SERVES 6

Method

Preheat the oven to 180C/360F. Cook the quinoa according to the instructions and then drain it. Place the onion, peppers, garlic, courgette (zucchini), beans, tomatoes and sweetcorn in a bowl and mix well. Add in the spices, oil and lime juice to the mixture. Scoop it in to an ovenproof dish or roasting tin. Add in the quinoa and mix well. Transfer it to the oven and bake for 40 minutes. Remove the dish from the oven and sprinkle the cheese on top. Return it to the oven and cook for another 5-10 minutes, or until the cheese is bubbling. Serve with a heap of green salad.

31

Pancetta Risotto

Ingredients

- 250g (8oz) Arborio rice
- 125g (4oz) Brussels sprouts, outer leaves peeled and quartered
- 100g (3½ oz) diced pancetta
- 100g (3½ oz) kale
- 50g (2oz) crème fraîche
- 25g (1oz) Parmesan cheese, grated (shredded)
- 2 cloves garlic, crushed
- 2 leeks, washed and finely chopped
- 250mls (8fl oz) milk
- 150mls (¼ pint) vegetable stock (broth)
- Zest and juice of 1 lemon
- 1 tablespoon olive oil
- Sea salt
- Freshly ground black pepper

SERVES 4

Method

Preheat the oven to 180C/360F. In a large saucepan, heat the oil, add the pancetta, leeks, sprouts and garlic and cook for 3 minutes. Add the rice, stock (broth) and milk. Transfer it to an ovenproof dish and cover it with foil. Bake it in the oven for 30 minutes. Add in the kale, crème fraîche, lemon zest and juice. Cover it and return it to the oven for 10-12 minutes or until the rice is tender. Season with salt and pepper. Sprinkle with Parmesan and serve.

Cheesy Stuffed Peppers

Ingredients

- 250g (9oz) rice
- 125g (4oz) mushrooms, chopped
- 100g (3½ oz) Cheddar Cheese, grated (shredded)
- 50g (2oz) pine nuts
- 25g (1oz) Parmesan cheese, grated (shredded)
- 4 red peppers (bell peppers, deseeded and halved lengthways
- 4 tomatoes, chopped
- 4 spring onions (scallions), chopped
- 3 cloves of garlic, chopped
- 2 tablespoons olive oil
- A small handful of fresh parsley

SERVES 4

Method

Preheat the oven to 190C/380F. Cook the rice according to the instructions or alternatively use a pack of microwave rice. Heat the oil in a frying pan, add the spring onions, garlic, mushrooms and tomatoes and cook for around 5 minutes until they have softened. Add in the rice, Cheddar cheese, pine nuts and parsley and mix well. Place the peppers on a roasting tin and spoon some of the stuffing mixture into each one. Sprinkle the Parmesan cheese on top. Transfer it to the oven and cook for around 20 minutes. Serve and eat straight away.

Squash Couscous & Baked Eggs

SERVES 4

Ingredients

450g (1lb) butternut squash, peeled and chopped

75g (3oz) couscous

6 large eggs, beaten

1 onion, roughly chopped

1 red pepper (bell pepper), deseeded and chopped

1 courgettes (zucchini), diced

1 clove of garlic, finely sliced

3 tablespoons fresh parsley, chopped

300mls (1/2 pint) boiling water

2 tablespoons olive oil

Sea salt

Freshly ground black pepper

Method

Preheat the oven to 200C/400F. Place the couscous in a bowl and add in the boiling water. Allow it to absorb the water for around 10 minutes, and then fluff it up with a fork. Pour the oil into a roasting tin and add the squash, pepper (bell pepper), garlic and onion. Toss the ingredients in the oil. Transfer it to the oven and cook for 10 minutes. Add in the courgette (zucchini), and cook for another 10 minutes. Pour the beaten eggs into the roasting tin and stir. Return it to the oven and cook for around 15 minutes until the egg is golden. Stir well to break up the egg. Add the parsley and couscous and toss it in with the other ingredients. Season and serve.

Smoked Paprika Drumsticks & Roast Garlic

Ingredients

- 450g (1lb) chicken drumsticks
- 450g (1lb) small new potatoes
- 8 shallots, whole with skin on
- 1 green pepper, deseeded and chopped
- 1 whole garlic bulb, whole with skin on
- 1 teaspoon ground cumin
- 1 teaspoon smoked paprika
- 3 tablespoons olive oil
- 1 lemon, halved
- 1 large handful of fresh basil or parsley
- Sea salt
- Freshly ground black pepper

SERVES
4

Method

Pour the olive oil into a large ovenproof dish. Add the cumin, paprika and a squeeze of lemon juice. Add the potatoes, chicken and green pepper (bell pepper) and coat them in the oil and spices. Cut the garlic bulb in half widthways and add it to the dish. Add in the shallots and lemon. Season with salt and pepper. Transfer it to a large ovenproof dish and cook in the oven at 180C/360F for 45 minutes. Sprinkle on the herbs just before serving.

Herby Plaice Fillets & Roast Asparagus

SERVES 4

Ingredients

300g (11oz) tender-stem broccoli

4 plaice fillets

3 cloves of garlic, chopped

2 large handfuls of fresh herbs (oregano, parsley or basil)

1 large bunch of asparagus

1 lemon, cut into wedges

1 teaspoon lemon zest

2 tablespoons olive oil

Sea salt

Freshly ground black pepper

Method

Preheat the oven to 180C/360F. Pour a tablespoon of olive oil into a roasting tin. Add the garlic, broccoli and asparagus and toss it in the oil. Lay the fish on top of the vegetables. Drizzle a tablespoon of olive oil over the fish and vegetables. Sprinkle on the half of the chopped herbs, lemon zest and season with salt and pepper. Transfer it to the oven and cook for around 15 minutes, or until the fish is completely cooked. Toss the remaining herbs over the top and serve with a wedge of lemon.

Minced Steak, Leek & Potatoes

Ingredients

600g (1lb 5oz) potatoes, peeled and thinly sliced

500g (1lb) minced (ground) steak

100g (3½ oz) cheese, grated (shredded)

50g (2oz) butter

2 leeks, washed and sliced

½ teaspoon dried oregano

300mls (½ pint) hot beef stock (broth)

Sea salt

Freshly ground black pepper

**SERVES
4**

Method

Heat half the butter in a large saucepan, add the steak mince and brown it for a few minutes. Add in the leeks, oregano and stock (broth) and stir well. Bring it to the boil, reduce the heat and simmer for 10 minutes. Season with salt and pepper. Preheat the oven to 190C/380F. Spoon the mixture into a roasting tin or oven proof dish. Layer the potatoes on top and coat them with the remaining butter. Cover with foil and transfer it to the oven and cook for 45 minutes. Remove it from the oven and sprinkle the cheese on top. Return it to the oven until the cheese is bubbling.

Halloumi & Sweet Potato Bake

Ingredients

- 600g (1lb 5oz) sweet potatoes, peeled and diced
- 350g (1lb) halloumi cheese, cut into thick slices
- 15g (½ oz) pine nuts
- 2 cloves of garlic, chopped
- 2 onions, roughly chopped
- 1 handful of fresh basil, chopped
- 1 red pepper (bell pepper), deseeded and chopped
- 1 yellow pepper (bell pepper), deseeded and chopped
- 2 teaspoons paprika

SERVES 4

Method

Preheat the oven to 200C/400F. Scatter the sweet potatoes, garlic, onions and peppers into a roasting tin. Sprinkle them with paprika and drizzle them in olive oil. Toss them well in the mixture. Lay the halloumi on top of the vegetables. Transfer it to the oven and cook for 25 minutes or until the sweet potatoes are tender and the halloumi is golden. Toss the basil and pine nuts through the dish before serving.

Lamb & Tomato Orzo Pasta

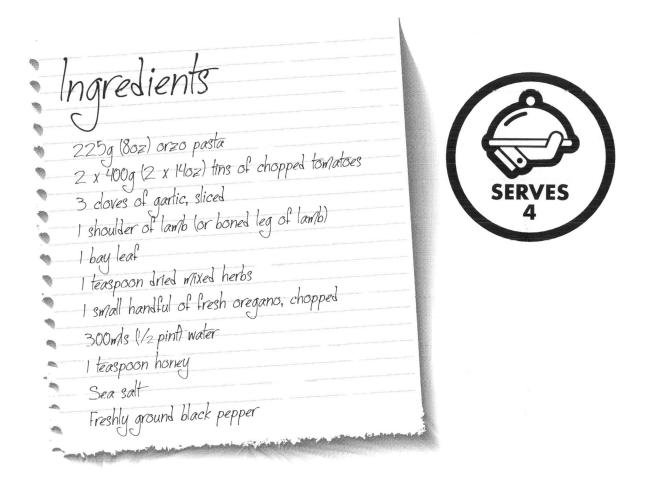

Ingredients

225g (8oz) orzo pasta

2 x 400g (2 x 14oz) tins of chopped tomatoes

3 cloves of garlic, sliced

1 shoulder of lamb (or boned leg of lamb)

1 bay leaf

1 teaspoon dried mixed herbs

1 small handful of fresh oregano, chopped

300mls (½ pint) water

1 teaspoon honey

Sea salt

Freshly ground black pepper

SERVES 4

Method

Preheat the oven to 180C/360F. Make small slits in the lamb and insert the pieces of garlic. Add the tomatoes, mixed herbs, oregano, bay leaf, honey, 150mls (¼ pint) water into a roasting tin and mix well. Place the lamb into the roasting tin and season with salt and pepper. To work out the cooking time, allow 25 minutes for every 450g (1lb) of lamb and add another 25 minutes. Around 20 minutes before the end of cooking, stir in the remaining 150mls (¼ pint) hot water and add the orzo. Stir well and return it to the oven to finish cooking. Allow it to rest for 10 minutes before carving and serving the lamb.

Mustard Pork Chops & Root Vegetables

SERVES 4

Ingredients

4 large pork chops, fat removed

4 medium potatoes, peeled and diced

2 large parsnips, chopped

2 large carrots, chopped

2 apples, peeled, cored and chopped

1 onion, roughly chopped

2 tablespoons olive oil

1½ tablespoons mustard

1 tablespoon honey

Method

Preheat the oven to 200C/400F. Toss the potatoes, apples, parsnips, carrots and onion into a roasting tin. In a small bowl mix together the olive oil and a tablespoon of mustard. Drizzle the mixture over the potatoes. Transfer it to the oven and cook for 25 minutes. In the meantime, place the pork chops in a hot frying pan and brown them on each side for around a minute. In a bowl, mix together ½ a tablespoon of mustard and a tablespoon of honey then spread the mixture onto the pork chops. Remove the roasting tin from the oven. Lay the chops on top of the vegetables and return it to the oven for around 20 minutes or until the pork is completely cooked. Serve and enjoy.

Salmon & Chickpeas

Ingredients

400g (14oz) tin of chopped tomatoes
400g (14oz) tin of chickpeas (garbanzo beans)
4 salmon fillets
1 clove garlic, chopped
1 teaspoon paprika
3 tablespoons olive oil
1 small handful fresh parsley, chopped

SERVES
4

Method

Heat the oven to 190C/380F. Scatter the chickpeas (garbanzo beans), tomatoes, garlic and paprika into a roasting tin. Add in the olive oil and mix well. Transfer it to the oven and cook for 10 minutes. Lay the salmon in the roasting tin on top of the vegetables. Return the tin to the oven and cook for around 15 minutes or until the salmon is cooked through and flakes easily. Sprinkle with parsley. Serve with crusty bread, rice or salad.

Prawns & Sweetcorn

Ingredients

450g (1lb) peeled king prawns (shrimps)

300g (11oz) cherry tomatoes

300g (11oz) sweetcorn

1 stick of crusty bread, torn into small pieces

4 tablespoons olive oil

1 tablespoon balsamic vinegar

2 handfuls of washed spinach leaves

Sea salt

Freshly ground black pepper

SERVES 4

Method

Preheat the oven to 220°C/440F. Scatter the crusty bread into a roasting tin and drizzle 3 tablespoons of olive oil over the bread. Scatter the tomatoes over the top. Cover the roasting tin with foil. Place it in the oven for around 20 minutes. Remove the foil and add the prawns and coat them in a tablespoon of olive oil. Return the tray to the oven and cook for 10 minutes. Scatter the spinach leaves and sweetcorn into the tin and stir in the balsamic vinegar. Mix together and return it to the oven for 5 minutes. Serve and enjoy.

Chilli Cheese Nachos

Ingredients

- 450g (1lb) lean minced beef
- 400g (14oz) tin of chopped tomatoes
- 2 x 400g (2 x 14oz) tins of kidney beans, drained and rinsed
- 75g (3oz) cheese, grated
- 2 red peppers (bell peppers), deseeded and chopped
- 3 cloves of garlic, peeled and chopped
- 2 onions, peeled and chopped
- 1 tablespoon medium chilli powder
- 1-2 teaspoons ground cumin
- 1 teaspoon dried oregano
- 1 beef stock cube
- 2 tablespoons olive oil
- 2-3 handfuls of tortilla chips

SERVES
4

Method

Preheat the oven to 180C/360F. Heat the oil in a saucepan, add the onion, garlic and mince and cook for 5 minutes to brown them. Transfer the mixture to a roasting tin or large casserole dish. Add in the chilli, cumin, oregano, beef stock cube and tomatoes and mix well. Return it to the oven and cook for 30 minutes. Add in the peppers and beans. Cook for 25 minutes. Scatter the tortilla chips over the chilli and sprinkle with cheese. Return it to the oven for a few minutes until the cheese has melted and bubbles. Can be served with rice, chunks of avocado and a heap of fresh salad. Enjoy!

Biryani Vegetable Rice

Ingredients

- 450g (1lb) basmati rice
- 150g (5oz) trimmed green beans, halved
- 3 tablespoons medium curry paste
- 1 medium cauliflower, broken into small florets
- 1 sweet potato, peeled and diced
- 1 red pepper (bell pepper), deseeded and chopped
- 1 onion, peeled and chopped
- 2 tablespoons olive oil
- 1 litre (1½ pints) vegetable stock (broth)
- Juice of 1 lemon
- A large handful coriander (cilantro) leaves, chopped

SERVES 8

Method

Preheat the oven to 200C/400F. Toss the cauliflower, sweet potato and onion into a large roasting tin and coat them in the olive oil. In a bowl, mix together the stock (broth) and curry paste. Add the rice, pepper and green beans to the roasting tin. Pour the stock over the rice and mix well. Tightly cover the roasting tin with foil. Bake in the oven for 35 minutes then check if the rice is tender and the liquid has been absorbed. If necessary, continue cooking until the rice has softened. Add the lemon juice and coriander (cilantro) into the rice and stir well. Scatter with coriander.

Herby Roast Vegetables

Ingredients

150g (5oz) cherry tomatoes, halved

150g (5oz) button mushrooms

3 celery stalks, chopped

3 cloves of garlic, peeled and chopped

2 carrots, peeled and roughly chopped

1 whole beetroot, washed and roughly chopped

1 large onion, chopped

1 courgette (zucchini), chopped

1 butternut squash, peeled and cut into chunks

1 teaspoon dried thyme

1 teaspoon dried oregano

1 large handful of fresh parsley

1 tablespoon olive oil

Sea salt

Freshly ground black pepper

SERVES 4

Method

Place all of the vegetables into an ovenproof dish. Sprinkle in the dried herbs, garlic and olive oil and toss all of the ingredients together. Season with salt and pepper. Transfer them to an oven, preheated to 180C/360F and cook for 30-40 minutes or until all of the vegetables are softened. Scatter in the fresh parsley just before serving.

Parma Wrapped Haddock & Roast Tomatoes

SERVES
6

Ingredients

600g (1lb 5oz) cherry tomatoes

18 green olives

6 haddock fillets

6 slices of Parma ham

1 onion, peeled and quartered

1 handful fresh parsley, chopped

1 handful of fresh basil, chopped

3 tablespoons olive oil

Method

Preheat the oven to 220C/440F. Pour the olive oil into a roasting tin and add the tomatoes and onion. Coat them in the oil. Transfer it to the oven and cook for 10 minutes. In the meantime, wrap each piece of fish in a slice of ham. Lay the haddock pieces on top of the tomatoes. Scatter the olives into the roasting tin. Return it to the oven and cook for around 15 minutes or until the haddock is cooked through. Sprinkle with basil and parsley. This is delicious with fresh crusty bread and a heap of fresh green salad.

Honey Roast Lamb & Root Vegetables

SERVES 4

Ingredients

2.25kg (5lb) leg of lamb

16 small potatoes, unpeeled

8 carrots, peeled and trimmed

8 small baby turnips, peeled

5 cloves garlic, crushed

2 teaspoons coarsely ground black pepper

1 large beetroot, peeled and cut into wedges

1 sweet potato, peeled and cut into wedges

1 teaspoon red chilli flakes

1 tablespoon chopped fresh rosemary

6 tablespoons olive oil

2 tablespoons balsamic vinegar

2 tablespoons honey

1 teaspoon sea salt

Method

Preheat an oven to 200C/400F. In a bowl, combine the garlic, chilli flakes, pepper, rosemary, balsamic vinegar, honey and 4 tablespoons of olive oil. Rub the oil mixture over the lamb, then season with a teaspoon of sea salt. Scatter the potatoes, beetroot, carrots, turnips, and sweet potato into a roasting tin and drizzle 2 tablespoons of olive oil over the top. Season with a little salt. Lay the lamb on top of the vegetables. Transfer it to the oven and cook for 20 minutes. Reduce the oven temperature to 170C/340F and continue cooking for around 90 minutes or longer if you prefer your lamb well done. Remove it from the oven and lamb rest for a few minutes before carving, covering the vegetables to keep them warm before serving.

Roast Egg & Chips

Ingredients

4 medium mushrooms, halved

2 baking potatoes, cut into wedges

2 large eggs

2 tomatoes

1 teaspoon paprika

2 tablespoons olive oil

Sea salt

Pepper

SERVES 2

Method

Preheat the oven to 180C/360F. Pour the oil into a roasting tin, add the paprika and potatoes and toss them all together. Season with salt and pepper. Transfer them to the oven and cook for 30 minutes. Remove them from the oven and add the mushrooms and tomatoes. Make 2 spaces for the eggs and crack them into the roasting tin. Return it to oven and cook for 7-8 minutes or until the eggs are firm. Serve and eat straight away.

Stuffed Butternut Squash

Ingredients

200g (7oz) cherry tomatoes

100g (3½ oz) feta cheese, crumbled

50g (2oz) pine nuts

2 large butternut squash, halved and seeds removed

2 onions, peeled and quartered

2 cloves of garlic, chopped

1 courgette (zucchini), diced

1 red pepper (bell pepper), diced

1 tablespoon Parmesan cheese

1 tablespoon parsley

1 teaspoon thyme, chopped

Pinch of cayenne pepper

3 tablespoons olive oil

SERVES 4

Method

Preheat the oven to 200C/400F. Place the garlic, 2 tablespoons of oil, cayenne pepper and thyme into a bowl and mix well. Coat the squash with the oil mixture. Lay the squash in a roasting tin, cut side up and transfer it to the oven. Cook for 35 minutes, or until the squash is tender. In the meantime, in a separate roasting tin, add the courgette (zucchini), red pepper (bell pepper), onion and drizzle a tablespoon of olive oil over the vegetables. Transfer it to the oven and cook for 20 minutes. Add the tomatoes and pine nuts to the vegetables and continue cooking for 10 minutes. Spoon some of the vegetable mixture into the squash. Sprinkle with, feta cheese, Parmesan and parsley. Return it to the oven and continue cooking for 5-10 minutes or until the cheese has melted.

Chicken, Broccoli & Pasta Bake

Ingredients

- 350g (12oz) leftover chicken or cooked chicken, chopped
- 250g (9oz) whole-wheat pasta
- 100g (3½ oz) cheese grated (shredded)
- 50g (2oz) broccoli florets, broken into small pieces
- 35g (1oz) cornflour
- 25g (1oz) Parmesan cheese, grated (shredded)
- 12 cherry tomatoes, halved
- 2 leeks, washed and thinly sliced
- 1 teaspoon dried oregano
- 450mls (15fl oz) milk

SERVES 4

Method

Preheat the oven to 190C/380F. Boil the pasta according the instructions on the pack. Drain and set aside 250mls (8fl oz) of the cooking water. Toss the pasta into an ovenproof dish and add the tomatoes, broccoli and chopped leeks. Add the cooked chicken to the dish. In a small bowl, mix together a tablespoon or two of the milk with the cornflour until it is smooth. Heat the remaining milk and cooking water in a saucepan. Gradually add the cornflour to the milk, stirring constantly until it thickens. Remove it from the heat and add the cheese, stirring all the while. Pour the cheese sauce over the pasta. Sprinkle the oregano and Parmesan on top. Transfer the dish to the oven and cook for around 20 minutes.

Curried Pork & Vegetables

Ingredients

400g (14oz) tin chickpeas, rinsed well

2 x 400g (2 x 14oz) tins of chopped tomatoes

4 pork steaks

3 cloves of garlic, chopped

2 carrots, peeled and chopped

2 red peppers, deseeded and chopped

1 green pepper, deseeded and chopped

1 onion, peeled and chopped

1 courgette (zucchini), sliced

2 tablespoons tomato purée

2-3 teaspoons curry powder

1 teaspoon chilli powder

1 teaspoon ground coriander

250mls (8fl oz) vegetable stock (broth)

2 tablespoons olive oil

Sea salt

SERVES 4

Method

Preheat the oven to 200C/400F. Toss the pork steaks, garlic, onion and carrot into a roasting tin and coat them in the olive oil. Transfer the tin to the oven and cook for 20 minutes. Add in the peppers, courgette (zucchini), chickpeas (garbanzo beans), tomatoes, tomato puree, curry powder, chilli, ground coriander (cilantro) and stock (broth) and mix well. Season with salt. Cook for around 35 minutes or until the sauce has thickened and the vegetables are tender. Can be served with rice, couscous or quinoa.

Tomato, Pomegranate & Feta Bake

SERVES 4

Ingredients

- 250g (9oz) brown rice
- 12 olives, stones removed
- 4 chicken quarters
- 2 yellow peppers (bell peppers), deseeded and chopped
- 2 cloves of garlic, chopped
- 2 lemons, cut into quarters
- 1 tablespoon plain flour
- 1 tablespoon fresh parsley, chopped
- ½ teaspoon saffron
- 750mls (1¼ pints) chicken stock (broth), hot
- 2 tablespoons olive oil

Method

Preheat the oven to 180C/360F. Place the flour in a bowl, add the chicken and coat it completely. Heat the oil in a frying pan, add the chicken, garlic and onion and brown them for 5 minutes then set aside. In a large jug, add the saffron to the stock (broth) and stir well. Transfer the chicken and onion to a roasting tin or ovenproof dish and add in the peppers, lemon quarters and rice. Pour in the stock and season with salt and pepper. Cover with foil and transfer it to the oven. Cook for around 50 minutes or until the chicken and rice is tender. Add in the olives for the last 5 minutes of cooking. Serve with a sprinkle of parsley.

Rosemary Lamb Chops & Garlic Potatoes

SERVES
4

Ingredients

- 1kg (2½ lb) potatoes, peeled and diced
- 225g (8oz) cherry tomatoes
- 50g (2oz) butter, softened
- 8 large lamb chops
- 6 sprigs of fresh rosemary
- 4 cloves of garlic, crushed
- 2 tablespoons olive oil
- 1 tablespoon balsamic vinegar

Method

Preheat the oven to 200C/400F. Heat the oil in a frying pan or flameproof dish. Add the lamb chops and brown them for around 2 minutes on each side. Remove the lamb chops and set aside. Scatter the potatoes, butter, garlic, rosemary and balsamic vinegar into the roasting tin together with the oil from the lamb. Coat the ingredients well. Transfer it to the oven and cook for around 20 minutes. Lay the lamb chops in the roasting tin, return it to the oven and cook for around 15 minutes. Toss the tomatoes into the dish and continue cooking for around 5 minutes. Serve and enjoy.

Spanish Lemon Chicken & Rice

Ingredients

- 250g (9oz) brown rice
- 12 olives, stones removed
- 4 chicken quarters
- 2 yellow peppers (bell peppers), deseeded and chopped
- 2 cloves of garlic, chopped
- 2 lemons, cut into quarters
- 1 tablespoon plain flour
- 1 tablespoon fresh parsley, chopped
- 1/2 teaspoon saffron
- 750mls (1¼ pints) chicken stock (broth), hot
- 2 tablespoons olive oil

SERVES 4

Method

Preheat the oven to 180C/360F. Place the flour in a bowl, add the chicken and coat it completely. Heat the oil in a frying pan, add the chicken, garlic and onion and brown them for 5 minutes then set aside. In a large jug, add the saffron to the stock (broth) and stir well. Transfer the chicken and onion to a roasting tin or ovenproof dish and add in the peppers, lemon quarters and rice. Pour in the stock and season with salt and pepper. Cover with foil and transfer it to the oven. Cook for around 50 minutes or until the chicken and rice is tender. Add in the olives for the last 5 minutes of cooking. Serve with a sprinkle of parsley.

Meatballs & Sweet Potato Wedges

SERVES 4

Ingredients

FOR THE MEATBALLS:

600g (1lb 5oz) beef mince

2 slices of brown bread, crumbled

3 tablespoons water

1 egg, beaten

1 clove of garlic, chopped

½ teaspoon onion powder/granules

FOR THE WEDGES:

1 kg (2¼ lb) sweet potatoes, washed and cut into wedges

6 large vine tomatoes, roughly chopped

2 onions, cut into wedges

1 handful of fresh basil, chopped

2 tablespoons olive oil

Method

Place the beef mince, egg, garlic, onion powder, breadcrumbs and water into a bowl and mix well. Shape the mixture into individual meat balls. Preheat the oven to 190C/380F. Pour the olive oil into a roasting tin, add the wedges, tomatoes and onion and scatter them in one layer. You may need to use 2 roasting tins to do this. Set the meat balls on top of the wedges. Transfer it to the oven and cook for around 20 minutes. Remove it from the oven and turn the meatballs over. Return it to the oven and continue cooking for around 25 minutes or until the wedges and meatballs are cooked through. Sprinkle with basil before serving.

Mozzarella, Ham & Vegetable Bake

Ingredients

400g (14oz) mozzarella cheese, sliced

200g (7oz) ham, roughly chopped

2 large potatoes, peeled and finely sliced

1 courgette (zucchini), finely sliced

1 onion, finely chopped

1 fennel bulb, finely sliced

1 red pepper (bell pepper), deseeded and sliced

A handful of fresh parsley, finely chopped

2 tablespoons plain flour

Salt and pepper

SERVES
4

Method

Preheat the oven to 180C/360F. Place the flour into a large bowl and season with salt and pepper. Toss the vegetables in the flour and make sure they are coated well. Scatter the vegetables in an even layer into a roasting tin and toss in some ham. Place a thin layer of mozzarella on top. Repeat for second and third layer, making sure you have enough mozzarella for the final topping. Cover with foil and transfer it to the oven. Cook for around 45 minutes. Remove the foil and cook for another 15 minutes and the top is golden. Serve and enjoy.

Roast Cod & Vine Tomatoes

Ingredients

450g (1lb) potatoes peeled and thinly sliced
25g (1oz) butter, softened
12 vine tomatoes, halved
4 thick cod fillets
2 garlic cloves, finely chopped
1 onion, sliced
Zest and juice of 1 lemon
1 red chilli, sliced
A large handful of fresh parsley, chopped plus more for garnish
4 tablespoons olive oil

SERVES
4

Method

Preheat the oven to 190C /360F. Scatter the potatoes and onion into a roasting tin, add the butter and one tablespoon of oil and mix well. Transfer it to the oven and cook for 20 minutes. In a small bowl, mix together 3 tablespoons of olive oil with the garlic, chilli, lemon zest and juice and parsley. Coat the cod steaks in the mixture and place them into the roasting tin, together with any remaining oil mixture. Scatter the tomatoes into the roasting tin. Return the tin to the oven and cook for 13-15 minutes or until the fish is cooked through. Serve with a sprinkling of parsley. Can be eaten on its own or with a leafy green salad.

One Pot Roast Chicken Dinner

Ingredients

- 700g (1lb 9oz) potatoes, peeled and quartered
- 100g (3½ oz) frozen peas
- 50g (2oz) soft butter
- 6 large carrots, peeled and roughly chopped
- 1 large chicken
- 1 onions, peeled and quartered
- 2 teaspoons dried mixed herbs
- 2 tablespoons olive oil
- 300mls (½ pint) chicken stock (broth)

SERVES 4

Method

Preheat the oven to 220C/440F. Cut any string off the chicken. Rub the butter and herbs over the chicken and season with salt and pepper. Lay the chicken in a roasting tin and surround it with the carrots, onion and potatoes. Pour the olive oil over the vegetables making sure they are completely coated. Transfer the tin to the oven and cook for 20 minutes. Reduce the heat to 180C/ 360F and continue cooking for 45 minutes. Add in the stock (broth) and peas. Continue cooking for another 15 minutes. Check that the chicken is completely cooked and serve.

Beef Stew

Ingredients

- 450g (1lb) lean braising beef steak, diced
- 400g (14oz) tinned chopped tomatoes
- 2 parsnips, peeled and cut into large chunks
- 2 carrots, peeled and cut into large chunks
- 2 cloves of garlic, peeled and chopped
- 1 potato, peeled and diced
- 1 stalk of celery, chopped
- 1 leek, chopped
- ½ swede, peeled and diced
- 1 teaspoon dried rosemary
- 1 teaspoon dried oregano
- 600mls (1 pint) beef stock (broth)
- 1 glass red wine (optional)
- 1 tablespoon olive oil
- 1 tablespoon Worcestershire sauce

SERVES 4

Method

Preheat the oven to 170C/ 340F. Heat the oil in a pan, add the beef and brown it for a few minutes. Or you can skip this step if you don't wish to brown the meat and save time. Transfer the beef to a roasting tin and add the carrots, swede, potato, garlic, celery, parsnips, leek and tomatoes. Stir well. Add in the wine (if using), rosemary, oregano, Worcestershire sauce and stock (broth). Cover the tin with foil and transfer it to the oven. Cook for around 2 hours, or until the beef is tender.

Chorizo & Balsamic Peppers

SERVES 4

Ingredients

- 1 large chorizo sausage, roughly chopped
- 4 cloves garlic, chopped
- 2 aubergines (eggplants), sliced
- 1 butternut squash, peeled de-seeded and chopped
- 1 red pepper (bell pepper), sliced
- 1 green pepper (bell pepper), sliced
- 1 yellow pepper (bell pepper) sliced
- 1 onion, chopped
- 1 teaspoon ground coriander (cilantro)
- 1 handful of fresh basil or marjoram, chopped
- 2 tablespoons balsamic vinegar
- 2 tablespoons olive oil

Method

Place all of the vegetables into a roasting tin and sprinkle in the coriander (cilantro), olive oil and balsamic vinegar. Apart from the fresh herbs, toss everything together and make sure it's well coated. Add in the chorizo sausage. Roast in the oven at 220C/425F for 25-30 minutes or until the vegetables have softened and are caramelised. Stir in the fresh herbs. Serve with a green leafy salad. As an alternative the vegetables can be topped with grated cheese.

Oven Baked Paella

Ingredients

400g (14 oz) tinned chopped tomatoes
300g (11oz) paella rice or Arborio rice
200g (7oz) chorizo, sliced
150g (5oz) peeled raw king prawns
75g (3oz) frozen peas
4 chicken thighs (skin on and boneless), cut in half
1 lemon, quartered
1 onion, peeled and chopped
1 clove of garlic clove, finely chopped
1 teaspoon smoked paprika
Pinch of saffron
600mls (1 pint) hot chicken stock (broth)
2 tablespoons olive oil

SERVES 4

Method

Preheat the oven to 200C/400F. Tip the onion and garlic into a roasting tin and add in the olive oil. Cook for around 10 minutes. Add in the tomatoes, paprika, stock (broth), and saffron and mix well. Add in the rice, chorizo and chicken. Season with salt and pepper. Return the tray to the oven and cook for 20 minutes. Add in the prawns and peas and return to the oven for 10 minutes until the rice is tender and the chicken and prawns are cooked through. Serve with a quarter of lemon and eat straight away.

Pomegranate &
Red Pepper Chicken

Ingredients

- 100g (3½ oz) passata or chopped tomatoes
- 4 handfuls of fresh spinach leaves
- 4 chicken breasts
- 2 red peppers (bell peppers), chopped
- Seeds from 2 pomegranates
- 2 onions, chopped
- 2 tablespoons balsamic vinegar
- 2 tablespoons olive oil
- ½ teaspoon ground cinnamon
- 1 handful of fresh coriander (cilantro) chopped

SERVES 4

Method

Place the olive oil, vinegar, passata/tomatoes and cinnamon into a bowl and mix well. Coat the chicken thoroughly in the mixture. Scatter the onions and peppers into an ovenproof dish and lay the chicken mixture on top. Cook in the oven for around 35 minutes at 200C/400F. Sprinkle on the coriander (cilantro) and pomegranate seeds. Scatter the spinach onto each of the plates and serve the chicken and vegetables on top. Eat straight away.

Lamb Shanks & Lentils

Ingredients

450g (1lb) puy lentils
4 lamb shanks
4 carrots, chopped
4 cloves of garlic, crushed
1 onion, finely chopped
4 tablespoons tomato purée (paste)
3 bay leaves
1 bouquet garni
1800mls (3 pints) beef or vegetable stock (broth)
4 tablespoons olive oil

SERVES 4

Method

Heat the oil in a large saucepan, add the lamb, turning occasionally until it is brown all over. Remove it and set aside. Add the onion, carrots and garlic to the saucepan and cook for 5 minutes. Return the lamb to the saucepan and add in the stock (broth), tomato purée (paste), bouquet garni, bay leaves and lentils. Transfer it to an oven-proof dish, cover and cook in the oven at 200C/400F for 2 hours. Check half way through cooking and add extra stock (broth) or water if necessary. Serve and enjoy.

Feta & Cannellini Bean Bake

SERVES 4

Ingredients

- 2 x 400g (2 x 14oz) tins of chopped tomatoes
- 2 x 400g (2 x 14oz) tins of cannellini beans, rinsed and drained
- 250g (9oz) plain (unflavoured) Greek yoghurt
- 200g (7oz) feta cheese, crumbled
- 2 clove garlic, crushed
- 1 small onion (chopped)
- 1 small handful of fresh basil, chopped
- 2 cloves garlic, chopped
- 1 teaspoon smoked paprika
- 1 tablespoon olive oil

Method

Preheat the oven to 200°C/400F. Pour the oil into an ovenproof dish and add in the onion, garlic, cannellini beans, tomatoes, basil and paprika. Season with salt and pepper. Transfer it to the oven and cook for 25 minutes. Remove the dish from the oven and stir in the yogurt. Scatter the feta cheese on top. Return it to the oven and cook for 15 minutes.

Roast Duck & Olives

Ingredients

12 x 400g (14oz) tins of chopped tomatoes
100g (3½ oz) olives
7 cloves of garlic, peeled and left whole
4 duck breasts
2 carrots, peeled and finely diced
2 sprigs of fresh thyme
1 large onion, peeled and chopped
1 teaspoon honey
Sea salt
Freshly ground black pepper
A handful of fresh parsley, chopped

SERVES 4

Method

Preheat the oven to 220C/440F. Place the tomatoes, onion, garlic, carrot, thyme and olives into a roasting tin. Stir in the honey and mix well. Season the duck breasts with salt and pepper. Lay them in the roasting tin. Transfer it to the oven and cook for around 45 minutes or until the duck is completely cooked. Sprinkle in the parsley. Serve with crusty bread and enjoy!

Maple Roast Cauliflower

Ingredients

8 parsnips, peeled and cut into lengthways

1 large cauliflower, sliced into florets, with the leaves

4 tablespoons olive oil

2 tablespoons maple syrup

A large handful of fresh parsley, chopped

SERVES 4

Method

Preheat the oven to 180C/360F. Pour a tablespoon of olive oil into a roasting tin. Place 3 tablespoons of olive oil in a bowl with the maple syrup and mix together. Coat the cauliflower and parsnips with the oil mixture. Season with salt and pepper. Scatter the vegetables into the roasting tin. Transfer them to the oven and cook for around 25-30 minutes or until the vegetables have softened. Sprinkle with parsley and serve.

Seafood & Vegetable Bake

Ingredients

600g (1lb 5oz) new potatoes, cut into wedges

350g (12oz) whole unpeeled raw prawns

75g (3oz) raw squid rings

6 cloves of garlic, peeled and chopped

4 tomatoes, chopped

2 large onions, cut into wedges

2 courgettes (zucchinis), roughly chopped

2 lemons, cut into wedges

3 sprigs of rosemary

2 teaspoons paprika

4 tablespoons olive oil

Sea salt

Freshly ground black pepper

SERVES 4

Method

Preheat the oven to 200C/400F. Parboil the potatoes for 5 minutes. Drain them and toss them into a roasting tin. Add in the olive oil, garlic, paprika, onions, courgettes (zucchinis), garlic, rosemary and lemons. Toss all the ingredients together. Transfer it to the oven and cook for around 30 minutes or until the potatoes have softened. Add the tomatoes, squid and prawns to the roasting tin and toss them in the juices. Return it to the oven and cook for around 10 minutes or until the prawns are completely cooked.

Pesto & Mozzarella Stuffed Mushrooms

Ingredients

125g (4oz) mozzarella, grated (shredded)

125g (4oz) diced ham

8 large mushrooms

2 tablespoons basil pesto

1 tablespoon olive

SERVES 4

Method

Preheat the oven to 200C/400F. Lay the mushrooms on a baking tray and pour a little olive oil onto each one. Sprinkle some of the ham onto each mushroom and drizzle some pesto sauce onto each one. Top it off with a sprinkling of mozzarella. Place them in the oven and cook for 8-10 minutes until the cheese is bubbling and hot. Serve with handfuls of leafy greens.

Pancetta, Apple & Sprouts

Ingredients

675g (1½ lbs) Brussels sprouts, trimmed and cut in half

125g (4oz) diced pancetta

4 sprigs of rosemary

3 apples, peeled, cored and sliced

3 tablespoons olive oil

A small handful of fresh parsley, chopped

SERVES 4-6

Method

Preheat the oven to 200C/400F. Toss the sprouts, apple, pancetta and oil together making sure everything is coated well with the oil. Add in the rosemary. Transfer it to the oven and cook for around 30 minutes or until the sprouts are tender. Sprinkle with parsley and serve.

69

Harissa Chicken Skewers & Roast Cauliflower

Ingredients

450g (1lb) chicken breast, diced

12 cherry tomatoes

1 large cauliflower

1 onion, peeled and chopped

1 teaspoon harissa powder

1 teaspoon smoked paprika

2 tablespoons olive oil

Sea salt

Freshly ground black pepper

SERVES 4

Method

Preheat the oven to 180C/360F. Place the chicken into a large bowl and add the harissa, smoked paprika and a tablespoon of olive oil. Coat the chicken completely in the mixture. Add a tablespoon of olive oil to a large roasting tin. Cut the cauliflower into slices. Scatter them in the roasting tin, together with the onion and coat them in olive oil. Thread the chicken chunks, onto skewers, alternating them with the tomatoes. Lay the chicken skewers in top of the cauliflower and season with salt and pepper. Transfer the roasting tin to the oven and cook for 25-30 minutes or until the chicken is completely cooked and the cauliflower is tender. Serve and eat straight away.

Vegetable Gratin

Ingredients

50g (2oz) Cheddar cheese, grated (shredded)

3 potatoes, peeled

3 large carrots, peeled

1 clove of garlic, peeled and finely chopped

1/2 butternut squash, peeled

1/2 swede, peeled

300mls (11fl oz) double cream

300mls (11fl oz) milk

Sea salt

Freshly ground black pepper

SERVES 4

Method

Preheat the oven to 200C/400F. Thinly slice the potatoes, squash, swede and carrots and place them in layers in a roasting tin or other oven proof dish. In a jug, combine the milk, cream and garlic and season it with salt and pepper. Pour the cream mixture into the vegetables. Scatter the grated (shredded) cheese over the top. Transfer it to the oven and cook for around 45 minutes or until the vegetables are all tender. Serve on its own or alongside meat and fish dishes.

Chilli Bean Bake

Ingredients

400g (14oz) chopped tomatoes
400g (14oz) haricot beans
125g (5oz) rolled oats
100g (3½ oz) peas
50g (2oz) Cheddar cheese, grated (shredded)
3 handfuls of spinach leaves
2 cloves garlic, crushed
1 onion, chopped
4 tablespoons olive oil
1 tablespoon soy sauce
1 teaspoon chilli flakes
1 teaspoon dried oregano

SERVES
4

Method

Heat the olive oil in a frying pan, add the garlic, onion, chilli and oregano. Cook for 5 minutes. Add in the chopped tomatoes, oats and beans and cook for 5 minutes. Stir in the peas, spinach and soy sauce. Transfer the mixture to an ovenproof dish and sprinkle with cheese. Bake in the oven at 200C/400F for 10 minutes until the cheese is bubbling.

Baked Tarragon Chicken

SERVES 2

Ingredients

225g (8oz) cooked leftover chicken

125g (4oz) peas

1 clove garlic, crushed (optional)

1 tablespoon fresh tarragon, chopped

300mls (½ pint) double cream or crème fraîche

Sea salt

Freshly ground black pepper

Method

Preheat the oven to 180C/360F. Scatter the chicken and peas in an ovenproof dish. Add the garlic (if using) and tarragon. Pour over the cream and season with salt and pepper. Transfer it to the oven and bake for 20 minutes, checking it is hot throughout. Serve with a salad or steamed mixed vegetables.

Cheesy Aubergine Bake

Ingredients

2 aubergines (eggplants) cut into 2cm slices

150g (5oz) feta cheese, crumbled

150g (5oz) mascarpone cheese

3 eggs

60mls (2fl oz) double cream (heavy cream)

4 tomatoes, sliced

2 tablespoons fresh oregano leaves, chopped

Sea salt

Freshly ground black pepper

SERVES 4

Method

Grease and line an ovenproof dish. Place the aubergines (eggplants) on kitchen roll and sprinkle with salt. Allow them to sit for 15 minutes then squeeze off the excess moisture. Preheat the oven to 200C/400F. Line the dish with the aubergine and tomato slices. Place the eggs, feta cheese, mascarpone cheese and double cream (heavy cream) into a bowl and using a hand blender mix until smooth. Pour the creamy mixture over the vegetables and sprinkle with oregano. Season with salt and pepper. Transfer it to the oven and bake for 25 to 30 minutes or until golden. Serve with a leafy green salad.

Lemon Chilli Chicken

Ingredients

8 chicken thighs or drumsticks

6 cloves of garlic, crushed

4 lemons, sliced in half with juice removed (keep the skins)

1 small chilli, deseeded and finely chopped

2 tablespoons honey

4 tablespoons fresh parsley

Salt & pepper

SERVES 4

Method

Place the chicken in a casserole dish. In a bowl place the lemon juice, chilli, garlic and honey. Mix it well. Pour the juice over the chicken. Put the lemon skins into the casserole dish next to the chicken and marinate for at least 1 hour (overnight is even better). To cook the chicken, transfer it to the oven and cook at 200C/400F for around 45 minutes or until it's cooked thoroughly. Sprinkle with parsley and season with salt and pepper. Serve with rice, quinoa or salad.

Tuna & Lentil Bake

Ingredients

200g (7oz) tinned tuna, drained

250g (9oz) lentils

50g (2oz) cheese, grated (shredded)

1 carrot, peeled and finely chopped

1 onion, peeled and finely chopped

1 small handful of fresh parsley, chopped

1 small handful of fresh chives, chopped

450mls (15fl oz) vegetable stock (broth)

1 tablespoon olive oil

SERVES 4

Method

Preheat the oven to 200C/400F. Pour the stock (broth) into a saucepan, add the lentils and cook for 12 minutes. Drizzle the olive oil into an ovenproof dish. Scatter the lentils into the dish and add the flaked tuna, onion, carrot and herbs and mix well. Sprinkle the cheese over the top. Transfer it to the oven and cook for around 20 minutes. Serve and eat straight away.

Desserts, Treats & Snacks

Citrus Bread & Butter Pudding

SERVES 6

Ingredients

75g (3oz) raisins

25g (1oz) honey or maple syrup

8 slices of whole-meal bread, crusts removed and cut into triangles

3 eggs

¼ teaspoon ground nutmeg

200mls (7fl oz) milk

100mls (3½ fl oz) double cream (heavy cream)

Juice of 1 orange

Butter for spreading and greasing

Method

Preheat the oven to 180C/360F. Grease an ovenproof dish with butter. Place the cream, milk, eggs, honey, nutmeg and orange zest into a bowl and combine them. Stir in the orange juice. Butter the bread and spread a layer into the ovenproof dish. Scatter raisins on top then add another layer of raisins and bread. Pour the milk mixture into the bread. Scatter the orange zest on top and sprinkle with nutmeg. Transfer it to the oven and bake for around 35 minutes or until the mixture has set and the bread is golden.

Lemon, Polenta Berry Bars

Ingredients

- 300g (11oz) frozen mixed berries
- 175g (6oz) caster sugar
- 175g (6oz) butter
- 150g (5oz) polenta
- 100g (3½ oz) ground almonds (almond meal/almond flour)
- 3 large eggs, beaten
- 2 teaspoons baking powder
- Juice of ½ lemon

MAKES 9

Method

Preheat the oven to 180C/360F. Grease and line a small baking tin. In a bowl, beat together the butter and sugar then add in the eggs and mix until creamy. Add in the polenta, almonds, baking powder, lemon juice and rind and mix well. Add in the berries and mix well. Transfer the mixture to prepared tin. Place it in the oven and cook for around 45 minutes or until golden. Transfer it to a wire rack and allow it to cool before cutting into pieces.

Blueberry Clafoutis

Ingredients

450g (1lb) ripe blueberries

125g (4oz) caster sugar

75g (3oz) plain flour

3 large eggs

1 teaspoon cinnamon

250mls (8fl oz) single cream

Butter for greasing

SERVES 4

Method

Preheat the oven to 220C/440F. Grease and ovenproof pie dish with butter. In a bowl combine the sugar, eggs, flour, cinnamon and cream and beat well until you have a smooth batter. Scatter the blueberries into the prepared dish. Pour the mixture over the top. Transfer it to the oven and cook for around 25 minutes or until it is golden. Serve with cream.

Cheesecake Brownies

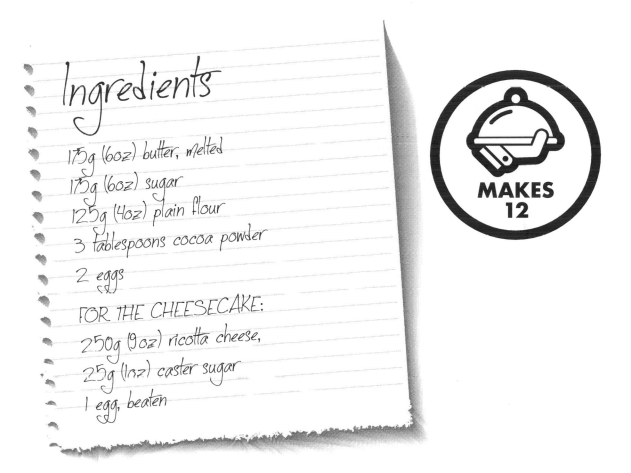

Ingredients

175g (6oz) butter, melted

175g (6oz) sugar

125g (4oz) plain flour

3 tablespoons cocoa powder

2 eggs

FOR THE CHEESECAKE:

250g (9oz) ricotta cheese,

25g (1oz) caster sugar

1 egg, beaten

MAKES 12

Method

Preheat the oven to 180C/360F. Grease a small baking tin. In a bowl, combine the melted butter with the cocoa powder and sugar. Stir in the beaten egg and mix well. Add in the flour and beat until smooth. Spoon the mixture into the prepared tin. In a separate bowl, beat the ricotta, egg and sugar for the cheesecake mix. Dollop the cheesecake mixture onto the chocolate mixture, then use a knife to make swirly patterns between the two mixtures. Transfer it to the oven and bake for around 40 minutes. Allow it to cool before cutting into pieces.

Chocolate Pudding

Ingredients

75g (3oz) butter
75g (3oz) caster sugar
50g (2oz) self-raising flour
50g (2oz) pecan nuts, chopped
25g (1oz) brown sugar
25g (1oz) cocoa powder
1 teaspoon cinnamon

1 egg
1 tablespoon honey
300mls (½ pint) black coffee, hot

SERVES 4

Method

Grease a small ovenproof dish with butter. Preheat the oven to 160C/320F. In a bowl, combine the flour, cocoa powder and cinnamon. Add the butter, caster sugar and egg and beat it well. Spoon the mixture into the greased oven dish. Sprinkle the pecan nuts and brown sugar over the top. In a jug, stir the honey into the coffee then gently add it to the pudding. Transfer it to the oven and cook for 55-60 minutes or until the pudding has set. Serve with cream or crème fraîche.

Spiced Baked Apples

Ingredients

50g (1oz) raisins
4 apples, peeled, cored and quartered
2 cinnamon sticks
Pinch of ground nutmeg
Grated zest and juice of 1 orange

SERVES 4

Method

Preheat the oven to 180C/360F. Scatter the apple into an ovenproof dish. Pour the orange juice over the top and sprinkle on the raisins, cinnamon and orange zest. Cover the dish with foil and transfer it to the oven. Bake for around 30 minutes, or until the apple is soft. Serve with whipped cream or crème fraîche.

Plum & Apple Crumble

Ingredients

25g (1oz) brown sugar
5 apples, peeled, cored and sliced
5 plums, stones removed and quartered
½ teaspoon cinnamon
50mls (2fl oz) apple juice

FOR THE CRUMBLE:
125g (4oz) flour
75g (3oz) butter, diced
50g (2oz) oats
50g (2oz) brown sugar
½ teaspoon cinnamon

SERVES 4

Method

Preheat the oven to 180C/360F. Scatter the plums, apples, apple juice and cinnamon in an ovenproof pie dish. In a bowl, rub together the butter and flour until it becomes crumbly. Add in the oats, cinnamon and sugar and mix well. Scoop the crumble over the fruit. Transfer it to the oven and bake for 30 minutes.

Fruit & Nut Squares

Ingredients

125g (4oz) butter
125g (4oz) raisins
75g (3oz) ground almonds
75g (3oz) jumbo oats
50g (2oz) hazelnuts, chopped
50g (2oz) dried cherries, chopped
25g (1oz) sesame seeds
1 egg, whisked
2 tablespoons honey

MAKES 9

Method

Preheat the oven to 180C/360F. Grease a small baking tin. In a bowl, combine the butter, egg and honey and mix until soft and creamy. Add in the fruit, nuts and oats and seeds and mix well. Spoon the mixture into the prepared tin and smooth it down. Transfer it to the oven and cook for around 20 minutes or until golden. Cut it into squares but let them remain in the tin until cool. Enjoy.

Baked Plums & Passion Fruit

SERVES
4-6

Ingredients

450g (1lb) plums, halved and stones removed

4 passion fruits, halved

1 teaspoon cinnamon

Method

Preheat the oven to 180C/360F. Place the plums into an ovenproof dish with the cut side facing up. Sprinkle the plums with cinnamon. Transfer them to the oven and bake for 25 minutes. Spoon the passion fruit seeds over the plums and return them to the oven for around 3 minutes to warm it slightly. Serve with cream or crème fraîche.

Apricot Flapjacks

Ingredients

150g (5oz) rolled oats

125g (4oz) butter, melted

100g (3½ oz) brown sugar

75g (3oz) dried apricots, chopped

MAKES approx. **12**

Method

Preheat the oven to 190C/380F. Grease a rectangular ovenproof dish with butter. In a bowl, combine the oats, sugar and apricots. Pour the melted butter over them and mix well. Scoop the mixture into the prepared dish and smooth it down. Transfer it to the oven and cook for around 20 minutes or until golden. Use a knife and cut into bars but leave it to cool in the dish, before removing.

Spicy Roast Chickpeas

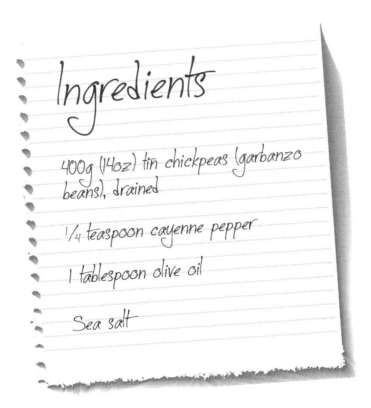

Ingredients

400g (14oz) tin chickpeas (garbanzo beans), drained

1/4 teaspoon cayenne pepper

1 tablespoon olive oil

Sea salt

Method

Place the olive oil, salt and cayenne pepper into a bowl and stir well. Add the chickpeas (garbanzo beans) to the bowl and coat them in the olive oil mixture. Spread the chickpeas on a baking sheet. Transfer them to the oven and bake at 220C/425F and cook for 30 minutes or until golden. Enjoy as an anytime snack.

Parmesan Kale Chips

MAKES
approx. **12**

Ingredients

50g (2oz) Parmesan cheese, grated

1 bunch kale, stalks removed and chopped

1 teaspoon brown sugar

½ teaspoon salt

2 tablespoons olive oil

Juice of ½ lime

Method

Preheat the oven to 180C/360F. Place the kale in a bowl. Pour in the oil and add the sugar and salt. Completely coat the kale in the oil. Scatter the kale in a single layer on a baking tray or roasting tin. Transfer it to the oven and cook for 5 minutes, then turn the leaves over and return them to the oven for around 7 minutes or until the kale is crisp. Sprinkle the parmesan and lime juice over the top.

You may also be interested in other titles by
Erin Rose Publishing
which are available in both paperback and ebook.

 Quick Start Guides

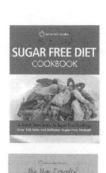

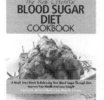

Books by Sophie Ryan
Erin Rose Publishing

30 Simple And Delicious Superfood Energy Balls And Bites
Recipes For Great Health and Wellbeing

Over 30 Easy And Delicious Superfood Energy Bars
Recipes To Boost Your Vitality

30 Simple And Tasty Energy Shots And Smoothies
To Power Up Your Health And Well-Being

Printed in Great Britain
by Amazon